Nicolaus Copernicus:
A Short Biography

The Astronomer
Who Moved the Earth

Doug West, Ph.D.

Nicolaus Copernicus: A Short Biography
The Astronomer Who Moved the Earth

Copyright © 2018 Doug West
ISBN: 9781980716556

All Rights Reserved. No part of this book may be reproduced in any form without written permission from the author. Reviewers may quote brief passages in reviews.

Table of Contents

Preface 1

Introduction 2

Chapter 1 - Childhood and Family 4

Chapter 2 - Education 7

Chapter 3 - Political and Administrative Career 14

Chapter 4 - The Heliocentric Theory 19

Chapter 5 - A Revolutionary Book 27

Chapter 6 – Death and Legacy 36

Timeline 41

References and Further Reading 45

Acknowledgments 46

About the Author 47

Additional Books by Doug West 48

Index 51

Preface

Welcome to the book, *Nicolaus Copernicus: A Short Biography*. This book is part of the 30 Minute Book Series and, as the name of the series implies, if you are an average reader this book will take around 30 minutes to read. Since this short book is not meant to be an all-encompassing biography of Nicolaus Copernicus, you may want to know more about this man and his accomplishments. To help you with this, there are several good references at the end of this book. Thank you for purchasing this book, and I hope you enjoy your time reading about the astronomer who changed man's view of the cosmos.

Doug West
April 2018

Introduction

Nicolaus Copernicus was a brilliant mathematician and astronomer who lived during the Renaissance and Reformation eras and contributed to science with a new model of the universe that placed the Sun, instead of the Earth, at the center of the universe. Although a similar theory had been formulated centuries earlier by Aristarchus of Samos, Copernicus went much farther than anyone before him. A major milestone in the history of science, the publication of his book, *De revolutionibus orbium coelestium (On the Revolutions of Heavenly Spheres)* in 1543 was a radical act that demolished thousand-year old beliefs.

Born in Royal Prussia, Nicolaus Copernicus held a doctorate in canon law and was also a classics scholar, governor, diplomat, translator, and physician besides being an influential mathematician and astronomer. He made valuable contributions to many fields, including economics, where he formulated a principle that would later become Gresham's law. Copernicus's daring and novel writings made all former theories about the system of the universe explode and put humanity on a new scientific path, eventually making way for the Scientific Revolution.

Copernicus's heliocentric theory led to such far-reaching consequences that it can be considered one of the main ideas that consolidated the foundation of modern science. Moreover, removing the Earth from the center of the universe was a shocking attack on humanity's system of beliefs. Because the Earth was now just a planet like any other, it meant that the belief in a correspondence between man and the surrounding universe and between microcosm and macrocosm was not justified, nor valid. With his courage to advance controversial theories, Copernicus changed humanity's conception of the universe and its place in it.

Chapter 1 - Childhood and Family

"Therefore, having obtained the opportunity from these sources, I too began to consider the mobility of the earth." - Nicolaus Copernicus

Historians now label the middle of the fifteenth century as the "Age of Discovery," as this was the period when the world would grow more closely linked and known. A heightened understanding of geography and astronomy yielded new methods of navigation. Mariners now took with them more refined navigation instruments, such as the quadrant and the astrolabe. Sturdier ships were being built and enhanced sailing techniques allowed explorers to travel to distant ports that were out of their reach just a generation before. This new era of travel greatly expanded commerce between Europe, Africa, Asia, and eventually the New World. Also spreading were new ways of thinking and viewing the world. Civilization was on the verge of changes that would shake the foundations of the long held beliefs and superstitions of the ancients that had held sway for over a millennium. Born into this rapidly changing landscape was a Polish boy by the name of Nicolaus Copernicus.

Nicolaus Copernicus was born on February 19, 1473, in Thorn (now Torun), a small city on the Vistula River, near the Baltic coast in the province of Royal Prussia, a Polish territory at the time. Copernicus himself described Torun as "this very remote corner of the Earth in which I live." His mother, Barbara Watzenrode, was the daughter of a wealthy merchant and city councilor from Torun while his father, Nicolaus Copernicus, Sr., was a well-to-do copper merchant from Cracow. Both his parents were German speakers from families of German heritage. Nicolaus and his three older siblings grew up with German as their mother tongue. However, at the time of Copernicus's birth, Torun had already become part of the Kingdom of Poland, which made him and his siblings Polish citizens, with German as their first language.

Nicolaus Copernicus, Sr., was actively involved in politics at a time of great turmoil for Prussia and Poland, taking the role of diplomat in important negotiations meant to keep Royal Prussia within the Kingdom of Poland. Through the extended family of his mother, Copernicus was related to many other wealthy and prominent Polish noble families of Prussia. Biographers believe that Copernicus spoke Latin, German, Polish, Greek, and Italian. Most of Copernicus's surviving works are in Latin, as that was the official language of the Roman Catholic church, Poland's royal court, and academia in Europe.

Figure – Portrait of Nicolaus Copernicus.

Chapter 2 - Education

"I am aware that a philosopher's ideas are not subject to the judgment of ordinary persons, because it is his endeavor to seek the truth in all things, to the extent permitted to human reason by God." - Nicolaus Copernicus

Copernicus's father died when he was ten years old, and his maternal uncle, Lucas de Watzenrode, immediately took Copernicus under his protection and made sure to personally supervise his education and career. Watzenrode wanted his nephew to receive an outstanding education and, discovering his academic potential, hoped that young Nicolaus would become a church canon. Although there are no surviving documents on Copernicus's childhood and early education, he probably attended St. John's School in Torun and later the Cathedral School at Włocławek.

In 1491, Copernicus enrolled at the University of Cracow (now Jagiellonian University). At the time, Cracow was one of the most vibrant cultural cities of Europe and a highly effervescent academic center. During the next four years, Copernicus studied in the Department of Arts at the Cracow School of Astronomy and

Mathematics, where he acquired a foundation of scientific and mathematical knowledge. In this period, he discovered the works of Albert Brudzewski, a professor of Greek philosophy at the university who taught private lessons on astronomy. Biographers agree that Copernicus regularly attended lectures on astronomy by renowned professors. Mathematical astronomy was thoroughly taught at the university, where the offer of studies included arithmetic, geometric optics, computational astronomy, and cosmography. Mathematical techniques were essential for those studying the stars.

Copernicus also acquired at university an extensive knowledge of philosophy and natural sciences, studying the writings of Aristotle and Averroes. Besides the formal, official academic offerings, Copernicus broadened his horizon by engaging in independent study. He read extensively outside his academic duties and began collecting books on astronomy. During these years, he made his first scientific commentaries. Because his interests varied greatly, he also attended courses on astrology and even painting.

Nicolaus Copernicus left the University of Cracow in 1495, without obtaining a degree. Meanwhile, his uncle had become Prince-Bishop of Warmia and wanted to place Copernicus in a vacant position in the local canonry. The plan didn't work out and eventually both

Nicolaus and his brother Andrew, who had studied with him at the university, were sent by their uncle to Italy, where they had to study canon law with the goal of easing their transition into ecclesiastic careers.

Figure – Courtyard of the Collegium Maius (Latin for "Great College") dating back to the 14th century at the Jagiellonian University in the historic part of Cracow, Poland.

In 1496, Copernicus enrolled at Bologna University, where he spent the next three years. Instead of focusing on canon law, he spent his time studying humanities and astronomy. He did receive his doctorate in law during his second trip to Italy in 1503, seven years after his first arrival to the country.

The Italian academic experience was undeniably valuable for setting Copernicus's path, mostly because in Italy he became the disciple of scientist and astronomer Domenico Maria Novara da Ferrara. Meeting Novara proved providential because the two men shared the same intense passion for astronomy, and their friendship was based on a continuous exchange of astronomical observations, ideas, and theories. It was indeed a fateful encounter, especially because, by getting to know Novara, Copernicus discovered that the traditional beliefs of his time could be challenged if one were daring enough. According to historian Edward Rosen, Novara didn't deter from arguing against Ptolemy, who was at the time considered the most advanced astronomer in history and whose theories were thoroughly embraced by the academic world and by society at large.

Being the leading astronomer at the University of Bologna, Novara had the responsibility of determining annual astrological prognostications on the fate of royal figures or influential Italian families from the city. Copernicus's contemporaries were interested in the arrangements of the stars, mostly because tables of planetary motions were essential for astrologers to establish horoscopes and periodic predictions of the future. Copernicus became Novara's assistant, helping in the issuing of the annual astrological prognostications while living in the same house as his master.

Since he assisted Novara and was directly involved in the making of prognostications, it is evident that

Copernicus had great knowledge of astrology and was familiar with the common astrological practices, which is not unexpected since, at the time, astrology and astronomy were almost interchangeable. However, Copernicus's interest in astrology was minimal.

Most likely it was Novara who familiarized Copernicus with two significant books which set the path of his future astronomical work: *Epitoma in Almagestum Ptolemaei (Epitome of Ptolemy's Almagest)* by Johann Müller (also known as Regiomontanus) and *Disputationes adversus astrologianm divinatricenm (Disputations Against Divinatory Astrology)* by Pico della Mirandola. Both books were revolutionary in unique ways, arguing against traditionally held beliefs and proposing new perspectives in astronomy and astrology. To expand his knowledge of the science of the stars, Copernicus read the works thoroughly and discovered in the writings of Regiomontanus clues that would prove instrumental in the later development of his theories. The famous 15th century astronomer Regiomontanus presented the most rigorous alternative to the archaic model of the universe developed by Ptolemy, which Copernicus found very inspiring. On March 9, 1497, Copernicus verified some of his own commentaries on Ptolemy's theory of the Moon's motion by conducting an observation at Bologna. That night, he observed an occultation of the star Aldebaran (Alpha Tauri) by the Moon. He later recalled the event in *De revolutionibus orbium coelestium (On the Revolutions of the Heavenly Spheres)*, his major work.

While advancing his astronomical theories, Copernicus also engaged in thorough humanistic study, reading classic authors such as Pythagoras, Cicero, Plutarch, Heraclitus, Plato, and others. His main goal was to gain deeper insights into the ancient astronomical and cosmological systems. By being engaged in Italian academic life, Copernicus had the opportunity to remain acquainted with the most important developments of the day in all his areas of interest, including astronomy, astrology, philosophy, mathematics, medicine, and theology. However, he devoted most of his energy to a systematic study of ancient and contemporary astronomical works. Besides two lunar eclipse observations, he did not make extensive observations while in Italy, but he gathered enough data to be able to recalculate components of the assumed orbits of the Sun, Moon, and a few planets. Between 1497 and 1529, Copernicus published a collection of 27 astronomical observations.

Copernicus spent the entire year of 1500 in Rome, performing an apprenticeship at the Roman Curia during the great jubilee celebrations. His interest in astronomy remained as fervent as ever, and on November 5, 1500, he observed another lunar eclipse. Biographers believe that he gave some informal lectures on mathematics while in Rome, although the actual topics of his lectures remain unknown.

After a short return to Warmia to claim his post at the canonry, Copernicus went back to Italy under special leave of absence from the chapter and took up medical studies, this time at the University of Padua, where he stayed from 1501 to 1503. At the time, medicine and astrology were considered joint sciences, because of the belief that the stars influence the body's dispositions. As usual, Copernicus read extensively beyond his academic duties. Besides reading translations of Greek authors, he became familiar with the Greek language, most certainly because many important works on astronomy were available only in Greek. Scholars believe that while at Padua, Copernicus also acquired remarkable painting skills by engaging with the local community of artists. However, he only painted a self-portrait. In early 1503, Copernicus passed the final examinations at Ferrara and was granted the doctorate of canon law.

Chapter 3 - Political and Administrative Career

"For it is the duty of an astronomer to compose the history of the celestial motions through careful and expert study." - Nicolaus Copernicus

Copernicus was 30 years old when he left Italy and returned to Royal Prussia. He moved with his uncle to the Episcopal Palace at the Lidzbark-Warminski and quickly became the Bishop's physician and secretary. He also fulfilled diplomatic duties, accompanying his uncle to sessions of the Royal Prussian court and thus participating in all important diplomatic events of his time. Meanwhile, using his knowledge of Greek, he translated to Latin collections of verses and composed his own poetic works. In 1509, he published a book of aphorisms of the seventh century Byzantine poet Theophylactus Simocattes, dedicating the book to his beloved uncle.

After his uncle's death, Copernicus became *magister pistoriae*, or "provisions fund" administrator, responsible for administering the economic enterprises of Warmia, a position which provided him with the opportunity to enjoy a lifetime of financial independence. He then moved to Frombork, a remote town on the coast of the Baltic Sea, where he had been given a house by the chapter. Since Frombork (Frauenberg in German) was the economic and administrative center and one of the two political poles of the Warmia chapter, Copernicus was drawn again into politics. The Frombork canon cathedral appointment proved, however, very suitable for his needs and aspirations, and he kept the job until his death. Having secured financial means, he could devote most of his time to his studies for as long as he pleased.

Figure – The cathedral at Frombork, in northeast Poland, is largely unchanged from the time when Copernicus was a canon there. In the distance, a branch of the Vistula River flows into the Baltic Sea.

Although he had many responsibilities as a church canon, including collecting rents for the church's lands, securing military defenses, supervising chapter finances, and providing medical services to elderly canons, Copernicus devoted all of his free time to his most ardent scientific and academic preoccupations. Never neglecting his lifelong interest in the stars and seeking ways to expand his research, Copernicus soon discovered that at Frombork he could easily conduct astronomical observations. Besides his official residence, he purchased a second residence in one of the town's towers, where he built his own private observatory in 1513. While modest, the observatory gave him ample opportunities for research and he conducted there all observations between 1513 and 1516. There is a limited number of recorded observations of Copernicus, although he certainly made many more. He was interested in alignments, conjunctions of planets and stars, and eclipses, and he used instruments assembled after ancient models to improve the accuracy of his research. Not all of his observations provided him with correct or helpful conclusions. An example is his assumption that planetary orbits are perfectly circular, a theory which was later invalidated by the findings of German astronomer Johannes Kepler, who proved that planetary orbits have an elliptical shape. After observations of Mars, Saturn, and the Sun, Copernicus made many important discoveries that helped him revise certain aspects of his system in the following years.

Figure – 1873 painting titled "Astronomer Copernicus, or Conversations with God" by Jan Matejko. The painted depicts Copernicus atop his tower at Frombork—with the cathedral's spires in the background—observing the sky with his wooden rulers (right).

Between 1516 and 1521, Copernicus lived in Olsztyn Castle, taking a position as administrator of Warmia and spending his free time working on *Locationes mansorum desertorum (Locations of Deserted Fiefs)*, trying to inspire farmers to populate deserted fiefs and thus bolster the economy of the province. He also continued to act as a political and diplomatic agent, with increasing responsibilities during the Polish-Teutonic War. He remained a supporter of the Polish

Crown's interests and when the Teutonic Knights attacked Warmia, Copernicus fought to save the province from the siege.

During his political and administrative career, Copernicus was interested in launching a monetary reform. In 1517, he developed the quantity theory of money, a key concept in economics even today. In 1526, he wrote *Monetae cudendae ratio* (*On the Minting of Coin*), where he dwelt on the importance of money and formulated a theory that was later developed by Thomas Gresham and received the name of Gresham's law. Copernicus's recommendations were well received by the leaders of his time.

In 1537, Prince-Bishop of Warmia Mauritius Ferber died, and Copernicus entered the election for succession as one of four candidates. However, the candidacy was a pure formality as the decision had already been made in favor of Johannes Dantiscus. Although there are doubts, some believe that Copernicus was indeed ordained a priest since he participated in the election for the episcopal seat, a position which certainly required ordination. Even after his uncle's death, Copernicus remained on familiar terms with the elderly bishops of Warmia, to whom he offered his services as a physician.

Chapter 4 - The Heliocentric Theory

"Moreover, since the sun remains stationary, whatever appears as a motion of the sun is really due rather to the motion of the earth." - Nicolaus Copernicus

According to the beliefs of the era, based on the writings of Hipparchus and Ptolemy, in the system of the universe, all celestial bodies rotated around the Earth, even though the mathematics never fully supported this theory. A Greco-Roman mathematician and astronomer who lived in the second century A.D., Ptolemy developed a geometric planetary model that formed the foundation of European astronomy for centuries. Ptolemy strayed from previous celestial theories, such as those of Aristotle who believed that celestial bodies moved in a fixed circular motion around the Earth, and he formed a new model with eccentric circular motions and epicycles.

Other theories circulated as well. Greek astronomer Aristarchus of Samos proposed a heliocentric system as early as the third century B.C. He considered the Sun the central celestial body in the universe and believed that the Earth orbits the Sun. Around 1507, inspired by the works of Aristarchus, who was the first to ever advance the heliocentric theory, Copernicus had the insight that the tables of planetary positions could be calculated more accurately if it were to accept this theory, contrary to what everyone around him believed. Retrospectively, one of the major reasons Aristarchus's theory was completely dismissed, and Ptolemy's theory widely accepted by Copernicus's contemporaries, was the pressure exerted by the church. The Roman Catholic Church was highly influential in the era, and the idea of the Earth as the center of the universe fitted the theological dogma far better. Unsupported by mathematics, Ptolemy's theories of a geocentric system of the universe thus found roots in faith, not in scientific evidence.

From his early dabbling in astronomy, Copernicus had been critical of Ptolemy's ancient system, especially because it placed the Earth at the center of the universe. Copernicus's dissatisfaction with the Ptolemaic system of the heavens was not, however, a singular occurrence. Many other astronomers of the era expressed doubts that made Copernicus reconsider very seriously what he had learned. Partly disagreeing with both Ptolemy and Aristotle, Copernicus wanted to develop a new celestial system which would reconcile incongruences. The heliocentric theory had the potential to fix many unresolved issues if proven correct as Aristarchus claimed. In an early, unpublished version of his final work, Copernicus cited Aristarchus but later removed the reference, a weakness for which he cannot be blamed because unlike Aristarchus, who had only advanced the theory, Copernicus was determined enough to prove it using the rigor of mathematics. Moreover, Aristarchus's system was not entirely accurate, nor very detailed. On the other side, Copernicus's system proved much more comprehensive and precise, especially as he introduced an efficient method for calculating planetary positions. Although he found the idea of a heliocentric system in the works of Aristarchus, Copernicus took his time to fully embrace it. As he progressed in his research and his mathematical calculations became more complex and accurate, he realized that this assumption explained numerous issues that seemed impossible to reconcile according to Ptolemy's theories.

Some of the technical aspects of Copernicus's system also appear in earlier works by Islamic astronomers Naṣīr al-Dīn al-Ṭūsī and Ibn al-Shāṭir, who considered the possibility of heliocentrism but eventually abandoned it. It is certain, however, that Copernicus did not have access to their works, which hadn't yet been translated from Arabic, and that he reached similar conclusions by independent means.

Scholars agree that by 1508, Copernicus had already developed a basic form of his celestial model, working around his theory of a heliocentric planetary system. Besides being convinced that the Sun, and not the Earth, was at the center of the solar system, he also believed that depending on the distance from the Sun, the orbit of each planet has a different size and speed. Moreover, he thought that the apparent daily rotation of the stars was a consequence of the Earth's rotation on its own axis. Copernicus supported this hypothesis by arguing that if the Earth is assumed to be in motion, it would be easy to establish an orderly relationship between the major planets and stars. By suggesting that the planets move in circular orbits, Copernicus showed that some of the mathematical devices that Ptolemy used to sustain his geocentric theory were very frail. However, he was also wrong in believing in circular orbital paths, but that remains his only major error.

For Copernicus, the idea of an orderly universe where celestial bodies form an interdependent whole was the main scientific criterion to respect while developing his research. Although he never deviated from this idea, the fact that he based some of his work on observations from antiquity whose validity he could not test made him unable to fix all the contradictions raised by his theory. This was another reason why he had to postpone the publication of his theories for many years.

Copernicus's heliocentric theory came with other major implications. One such implication was that the stars' fixed positions should display a small periodic change, known as parallax, as the Earth orbits the Sun. Because he couldn't measure the small periodic change in the stars' positions, Copernicus concluded that the change wasn't obvious because the stars were far too distant for people to detect the change. Accepting his theory meant also accepting that the universe was much larger than people had previously believed.

Figure – Copernicus' great book *Revolutions* contains a diagram that overturns all previous conceptions of the Universe. The central position is occupied not by the Earth, but by the Sun (Sol). The Sun is orbited by the planets Mercury, Venus, Earth (with the Moon in orbit), Mars, Jupiter, Saturn, and the sphere of the stars.

By 1514, Copernicus had already written an outline of his heliocentric theory, *Nicolai Copernici de hypothesibus motuum coelestium a se constitutis commentariolus*—commonly referred to as the *Commentariolus* ("Little Commentary"). It was only a sketch that provided an early iteration of the hypothesis of a heliocentric system and included a short description without the mathematical apparatus. Although brief, the work was one of the most radical ever written because it enforced the idea that the Earth was a just a planet like any other, revolving around the Sun, and not the center of the universe as theology, tradition, and ancient science proclaimed.

The 40-page manuscript provided a summarization of the main theoretical principles of the heliocentric system and indicated that they would later be accompanied by mathematical devices as evidence. Each hypothesis from the summary alluded to an important and revolutionary aspect of the new celestial model. Besides declaring that the Sun, and not the Earth, was at the center of the universe, *Little Commentary* also suggested, among others, that: all celestial bodies rotate around the Sun; the stars don't move and only seem to because the Earth is rotating; the Earth's orbit is a sphere; the stars are vastly further from the Sun than the Earth; and the Earth's movement makes other planets appear as if they were moving in an opposite direction. Copernicus emphasized the value of his work in calculating new and more accurate planetary tables. He also declared himself an admirer of Ptolemy and his scientific tradition, even though his work fundamentally opposed that of his famous predecessor. *Little Commentary* also stated that the Earth's daily rotation on its axis and its yearly revolution around the Sun cause the daily motion of the stars and the annual motion of the Sun.

Reluctant to make his theories public, Copernicus shared a few manuscript copies of *Little Commentary* with his closest friends and acquaintances, mostly astronomers with whom he had collaborated at the University of Cracow. His friends were familiar with his preoccupations and witnessed his development over the years. Although he received little direct feedback for *Little Commentary*, Copernicus gained the attention of contemporary scholars and scientists who began to closely follow the progress of his unconventional ideas. An evident proof that Copernicus had already established himself as a respectable astronomer within and outside local Polish communities by that time is the fact that in 1514 he was invited to take part in the discussions concerning the reform of the calendar at the church's Fifth Lateran Council. The calendar in common usage at the time was still the one produced under the reign of Julius Caesar, and over the centuries it had become out of alignment with the actual position of the Sun and the changing of the seasons. Whether

Copernicus offered assistance on the reform of the calendar is in question, however, because he did not attend any of the council's sessions.

In 1533, Johann Albrecht Widmannstetter, secretary to Pope Clement VII, presented Copernicus's heliocentric theory to the Pope in a series of public lectures. The Pope was pleased with the findings and everyone showed an interest in Copernicus and his work. In 1536, a cardinal from Rome, Nikolaus von Schönberg, wrote a letter to Copernicus, urging him to make his theory known to scholars as soon as possible and to send the Cardinal all his writings on the subject. When the letter reached Copernicus, his major work was near its final form, and educated people from all corners of Europe had heard rumors about it. Copernicus ignored, however, the formal request because he still had some hesitations.

Chapter 5 - A Revolutionary Book

"Finally we shall place the Sun himself at the center of the Universe." - Nicolaus Copernicus

Around 1532, Copernicus completed his work on the groundbreaking manuscript of *On the Revolutions of the Heavenly Spheres*, which aimed to introduce to the world his heliocentric theory. After the brief overview provided in *Little Commentary*, which circulated only among Copernicus's acquaintances, the final work was supposed to thoroughly cover all of the main principles of the theory in a detailed form.

Despite pressure from various directions, Copernicus did not hurry to publish the book, perhaps out of fear of religious, philosophical, and astronomical objections. Although many insisted he should make his discovery public, Copernicus feared that the novelty and incomprehensibility of his findings would expose him to the ridicule of society. Most probably, Copernicus feared that a theory that removed the Earth from the center of the universe would be considered heretical. His fears were justified, considering that many theologians contested him for a very long time and that later supporters of the heliocentric theory, such as

Galileo Galilei and Giordano Bruno, suffered persecution for their beliefs.

Aware that his theories flagrantly opposed the teachings of the Bible, Copernicus delayed the publication of his book. He believed that people ignorant of mathematics twisted the meaning of the Bible to fit their superstitious beliefs, disregarding any scientific proof. While he was willing to stand against them, he needed to make sure that he had made enough observations and gathered enough scientific evidence to back up his theories before going public.

The road to publication was thus long. In 1539, Copernicus was still making minor changes to improve *Revolutions* when he received the visit of a 25-year-old mathematician from Austria, Georg Joachim Rheticus. Enthusiastic and spirited, Rheticus decided he wanted to meet Copernicus after hearing rumors about his daring theories. He became Copernicus's pupil, staying with him for two years and voluntarily taking the responsibility of being his assistant and writing his biography. Unfortunately, the biography was lost.

Shortly after Rheticus's arrival, he and Copernicus wrote a book titled *Narratio prima (First Account)*, in which they gave an outline of the essential principles of the heliocentric theory. A joint effort of the two great minds, *First Account* put special emphasis on the value of Copernicus's work in the calculation of new planetary tables and less on the philosophical implication of a new celestial arrangement where the Sun would be central. Although they expected objections, Copernicus and Rheticus knew that the theory offered an effective method for understanding the order of the planets and for calculating the relative distances between the Sun and the planets, and that that was very valuable for the scientific community. *First Account* appeared, however, not under Copernicus's name but under that of Rheticus. They saw its publication as a trial for what would be the release of the main work.

In 1542, some chapters from *Revolutions* appeared in a treatise on trigonometry by Copernicus, who, incessantly pressured by Rheticus, had finally acquiesced to publishing some of his writings. Since the overall reception of the work was favorable and Rheticus continued to insist that the important work be published, Copernicus ultimately agreed. In the preface to *Revolutions*, Copernicus revealed that he chose to withhold the publication of his work for 36 years.

Revolutions was very complex and comprised six sections, which Copernicus wanted to be regarded as a mathematical reinterpretation of Ptolemy's work. Copernicus also hoped his work would offer future astronomers the means to make more accurate predictions that could be used in calendar reform, and that would explain the mysterious variations of the planets' velocity, brightness, and retrogressions with a simpler geometric configuration. In the first section of the book, Copernicus introduced his mathematical arguments against established theories, such as the fixed position of the Earth, and gave an overview of his observations regarding the right order of the planets. In the next section, he used the same mathematical arguments against phenomena attributed to the motion of the Sun. In the third section, he described the Earth's motion and explained equinoxes as being caused by the gyration of the Earth's axis. The last three sections dealt with the motions of the five other planets known at the time and the Moon.

Figure – Copernicus's great work, On the Revolutions of the Heavenly Spheres.

Since the circulation of *Little Commentary*, Copernicus had developed diagrams and mathematical calculations to support his arguments. Because the new manuscript contained complex tables and diagrams, Copernicus and Rheticus decided together to use the services of a German printer, Johannes Petreius from Nuremberg (now Nürnberg). At the time, Nürnberg was the leading printing center in Germany and Petreius was known for publishing numerous ancient and modern works on astronomy and astrology. Although Rheticus volunteered to personally supervise the publishing of the book, he was forced to leave the city before the job was completed and delegated his responsibilities to Andreas Osiander, a Lutheran theologian with influence on the political scene of the city. Rheticus trusted Osiander because he had experience in supervising the production and printing of mathematical books.

A follower of the German monk who instigated the Protestant Reformation, Martin Luther, Osiander couldn't accept Copernicus's theories and, going way beyond his duty, he added without permission a "letter to the reader" to the manuscript, in which he claimed that the book had no claim to truth and that the heliocentric theory was nothing other than an abstract idea. Osiander also claimed that the hypothesis of a stationary Sun was just a conventional device aimed at simplifying planetary computations. According to Osiander, "These hypotheses need not be true nor even probable. [I]f they provide a calculus consistent with the observations, that alone is enough." By leaving the introduction unsigned, Osiander led readers to assume that it had been written by Copernicus himself. This ended up weakening the appeal of the book because it discredited and negated its own premise, which was the reality of a heliocentric celestial system.

Rheticus felt an immense anger when he discovered the betrayal of Osiander, but his efforts to reprint the book without the scandalous introduction brought no results. Since the book was published shortly before Copernicus's death, he could no longer reveal the truth and defend his work. Astronomer Johannes Kepler revealed to the public the truth about the book's introduction in 1609, exposing Osiander. Kepler was also the one who developed further Copernicus's heliocentric theory, by expanding on the work, correcting errors, and adding new evidence.

Some historians argue that Osiander's introduction contributed to the positive reception of the book since it made it possible for readers to see it solely as a new device for calculating the planetary tables instead of seeing it as a radical philosophy aimed at fundamentally changing the way humanity saw the universe. Osiander unknowingly provided the best excuse so the book would not be considered a heresy by the church. Considering that the mathematical apparatus of the book was so advanced that only a few highly educated people in Europe could read it, there were few who could understand the magnitude of its consequences and contest it. The few people who could understand it agreed that the book rivaled in significance the works of Ptolemy.

Although Copernicus had crystallized his theory by 1510, his major work was thus published only in the year of his death, 1543. The original edition of *Revolutions* included only a few hundred copies, and many of them have survived to the present day. Some early handwritten drafts also survived. Decades after the publication of Copernicus's revolutionary book, there were still very few astronomers who approved his theory. Astronomers agreed that Copernicus's findings could be used efficiently in astronomical calculations without having necessarily to accept his heliocentric theory. Eventually, it was accepted that the Copernican system undoubtedly explains the motions of the planets and other astronomical phenomena with an unprecedented accuracy.

As Copernicus himself anticipated, the publication of his book led to waves of scandal and controversy, especially within religious circles. One of the first influential religious leaders to criticize Copernicus was Martin Luther, who was very vocal about his opposition to the heliocentric theory. The Protestant theologian went as far as to say that Copernicus was a "fool" who wanted to destroy the foundation of astronomy and accused him of disregarding the words of God as they are written in the Bible.

Unsurprisingly, the Roman Catholic Church also considered Copernicus's work entirely heretical. Copernicus dedicated the main work of his life, *Revolutions*, to Pope Paul III, perhaps in an attempt to soften the critical reception that he anticipated from religious leaders. Copernicus referred in the dedication to ancient writings of thinkers such as Cicero and Plutarch who went against tradition and advanced novel theories, hoping in the efficiency of an appeal to historical examples. Ironically, as the support for the book increased over the years, the Catholic Church felt threatened by its radical content and rapidly declared the heliocentric theory a condemnable heresy. Copernicus's attempts to dampen criticism would prove thus to be futile because the church banned his book in 1616. It was approved a few years later, but only after heavy editing of all passages that referred to a moving Earth or to the central position of the Sun. For decades, the book remained unavailable in countries with a strong Catholic influence. Only in 1835 did the Roman Catholic Church remove Copernicus's book from the list of banned writings.

While for Christians the views of Aristotle and Ptolemy had religious meanings attached to them and were respected as highly as any other religious dogma, there were scientists who thought that further scientific development wasn't possible without a critical view of past theories. For them, Copernicus represented a symbol of courage and intellectual integrity in the face of ignorance.

Chapter 6 – Death and Legacy

"Of all things visible, the highest is the heaven of the fixed stars." - Nicolaus Copernicus

Nicolaus Copernicus died on May 24, 1543, in Frombork, at the age of 70, after a bout of apoplexy and paralysis due to a stroke. According to a popular legend, he saw the first copy of his book while on his deathbed and clutched to it before dying peacefully. Copernicus never married and didn't have children. After his death, his former pupil, Georg Joachim Rheticus, became his successor.

Copernicus was buried below the floor of the Frombork Cathedral. The exact position of his body was not known until recently, when in 2005 archeologists excavated the floor of the cathedral in search of his body. The archaeologists found only scattered bones of a 60 to 70-year-old man. Experts at the Central Forensics Laboratory at the Warsaw police reconstructed the face and compared it with the best-known portrait of Copernicus, which hangs in the Town Hall in Torun. To further validate that the bones were truly that of Copernicus, DNA from a tooth fragment was extracted and compared to DNA from strands of hair found in one of the books from Copernicus's personal library, held at Sweden's Upsala University. The DNA samples matched—the grave of Nicolaus Copernicus had been found nearly five centuries after his death!

Figure – Statue of Nicolaus Copernicus in Warsaw, Poland.

Legacy

After Copernicus's death, his work was not immediately accepted and adopted; rather, it would be over two centuries later that his heliocentric model of the solar system would be widely accepted. Following Copernicus, the next great astronomer was the Dutchman, Tycho Brahe, born into a noble family in 1546. Brahe became interested in studying the stars and planets and the king of Denmark, Frederick II, funded Tycho with an elaborate observatory on an island between Denmark and Sweden. The telescope had not yet been invented, so all observations were conducted by the naked eye and large mechanical instruments to carefully measure the positions of the stars and planets. With the help of his aides, Tycho made extensive visual observations of the stars and planets from his observatory. Tycho's model of the solar system combined the geocentric and heliocentric models. The Earth was the center of the universe, with the Moon rotating round the Earth. The Sun also rotated around the Earth. In his model, the other planets, Mercury, Venus, Jupiter, and Saturn, and the fixed stars all rotated around the Sun.

A young German teacher named Johannes Kepler came to work for Tycho doing routine observations for the elder astronomer. Kepler didn't believe in Tycho's model of the universe; rather, secretly, he was a follower of Copernicus's view of the cosmos. After

Tycho's death, Kepler continued his master's work gathering more observations, and started to analyze the many observations that had accumulated over the years. Working primarily with observations of the planet Mars, Kepler developed three laws of planetary motion and refined the simple model of Copernicus, making the orbits of the planets about the Sun ellipses, not circles. Kepler's new formulation fit the observations much better than previous models and gave more accurate predicted positions of the planets.

Galileo Galilei made the next great contribution to the development of astronomy as a science and helped mankind discover the worlds beyond the confines of the Earth's atmosphere. His refinement of the telescope in 1609 led to observations of the heavens more closely than any other human had done in history. In his publication of the *Starry Messenger* in 1611, Galileo told the world of his observations of the phases of the planet Venus, the four moons of Jupiter, and many other observations. His observations clearly pointed to the Earth as the center of the solar system. Unfortunately, Galileo's observations and their implications provoked certain clerics high up in the Catholic Church. In 1616, after an investigation by theologians of the Holy Office of the Roman Inquisition, Galileo was told that the "doctrine of Copernicus…cannot be defended or held."

Born in the year of Galileo's death, 1642, the English scientist Sir Isaac Newton would bring together in an elegant form the laws of motion and gravitation explaining the movement of the planets around the Sun. In 1687, Newton published his seminal work, the *Mathematical Principles of Natural Philosophy*, in which he argued that gravitation, or the mutual attraction between all bodies, controlled the motion of falling objects and the movement through the sky of heavenly bodies. Sir Isaac Newton's mathematical genius won him immediate renown in England and he was showered with honors. By the middle of the eighteenth century, the Earth had moved from the center of the universe to be the third planet from the Sun. Gone was the rigid world view of Aristotle and Ptolemy, replaced with the enlightenment brought on by the Scientific Revolution and the work of Nicolaus Copernicus.

The End

I want to thank you for purchasing this book, and I hope you enjoyed reading it. Please don't forget to leave a review as I read every one of them and they help me become a better writer.

-Doug

Timeline

February 19, 1473 – Nicolaus Copernicus is born in Thorn (Torun), a small town in Royal Prussia, part of the Kingdom of Poland.

1483 – Copernicus's father dies.

1491 – Copernicus enrolls at the University of Cracow to study liberal arts.

1495 – Leaves the university, without getting a degree.

1496 – Starts to attend courses at Bologna University in Italy.

1497 – Meets astronomer Domenico Maria de Novara and becomes his disciple and assistant.

March 9, 1497 – Makes his first major observation of the Moon eclipsing the bright star Aldebaran.

1500 – Copernicus moves to Rome where he takes a position as an apprentice at the Roman Curia.

November 5, 1500 – Observes a lunar eclipse.

1501 – Copernicus returns to Frombork from Italy to request a leave of absence to continue his studies abroad. After securing permission from the Warmian chapter, he goes to Padua to study medicine.

1501 – 1503 – Studies medicine at the University of Padua.

1503 – Passes his final examinations at the University of Ferrara, obtains his doctorate of canon law, and returns to Royal Prussia.

1504 – Becomes his uncle's physician and secretary, living in the Episcopal Palace at Lidzbark.

1507 – Has the idea of a heliocentric celestial system.

1508 – Develops a basic form of his heliocentric model.

1509 – Publishes a translation of Greek verses, dedicating the book to his beloved uncle.

1512 – After his uncle's death, Copernicus is appointed church canon in Frombork.

1512 (approximate) – Copernicus writes an outline of the heliocentric theory, *Little Commentary*, and shares the manuscript with his friends and acquaintances.

1513 – Builds his own private observatory to expand his astronomical research.

1514 – The church invites Copernicus to give his opinion regarding a possible calendar reform.

1517 – Copernicus develops the quantity theory of money.

1526 – Writes *On the Minting of Coin*, in which he formulates an innovative principle of economics.

1532 – Copernicus completes his work on the manuscript that would make him famous, *On the Revolutions of the Heavenly Spheres.*

1533 – Pope Clement VII hears about Copernicus's theories during a series of public lectures.

1536 – Cardinal Nikolaus von Schönberg writes to Copernicus, urging him to publish his writings as quickly as possible, but he still hesitates.

1539 – Copernicus receives the visit of Georg Joachim Rheticus, a scientist and astronomer from Austria who wants to become his disciple.

1540 – Copernicus and Rheticus publish *First Account*, a summary of the heliocentric theory.

1542 – Chapters of *Revolutions* appear in a treatise on trigonometry, but Copernicus still hesitates when pressured to publish the full manuscript.

1543 – Copernicus's main manuscript, on which he worked for 36 years, is finally published.

May 24, 1543 – Copernicus dies due to a stroke but manages to see a copy of his book before dying peacefully in his bed.

1609 – Johannes Kepler reveals the truth about the clandestine introduction to the *Revolutions* written by Andreas Osiander.

1616 – The Roman Catholic Church bans Copernicus's writings.

1835 – Roman Catholic Church removes Copernicus's book from list of banned writings.

2005 – After his grave had been unknown for years, it is rediscovered, and Copernicus is reburied in Frombork Cathedral.

References and Further Reading

Couper, Heather and Nigel Henbest. *The History of Astronomy*. Firefly Books Ltd. 2007.

Crowther, J.G. *Six Great Scientists: Copernicus, Galileo, Newton, Darwin, Marie Curie, Einstein*. Barnes and Noble, Inc. 1995.

Dreyer, John L. E. *History of the Planetary Systems from Thales to Kepler*. Cambridge University Press. 1906.

Gingrich, Owen. "The Copernicus grave mystery." *PNAS*. Vol. 106, no. 30, July 28, 2009.

Hall, John W. And John G. Kirk (editors). *History of the World: Earliest Times to the Present Day*. World Publications Group, Inc. 2005.

Volmann, William T. *Uncentering the Earth: Copernicus and the Revolutions of the Heavenly Spheres*. Atlas Books. 2006.

Internet Reference

Copernicus' Grave Found in Polish Church. November 3, 2005. USA Today. Accessed March 5, 2018. https://usatoday30.usatoday.com/tech/science/discoveries/2005-11-03-copernicus-grave_x.htm#

Acknowledgments

I would like to thank Lisa Zahn and Andreea Mihaela for help in preparation of this book. All photographs are from the public domain. The quotes at the beginning of each chapter are from Brainyquote.com.

About the Author

Doug West is a retired aerospace engineer, small business owner, and experienced non-fiction writer with several books to his credit. His writing interests are general, with expertise in science, history, biographies, and "How-to" topics. Doug has a B.S. in Physics from the Missouri School of Science and Technology and a Ph.D. in General Engineering from Oklahoma State University. He lives with his wife and little dog, "Scrappy," near Kansas City, Missouri. Follow the author on Facebook at https://www.facebook.com/30minutebooks.

Figure – Doug West (photo by Karina West)

Additional Books by Doug West

Buying and Selling Silver Bullion Like a Pro
How to Write, Publish, and Market Your Own Audio Book
A Short Biography of the Scientist Sir Isaac Newton
A Short Biography of the Astronomer Edwin Hubble
Galileo Galilei – A Short Biography
Benjamin Franklin – A Short Biography
The Astronomer Cecilia Payne-Gaposchkin – A Short Biography
The American Revolutionary War – A Short History
Coinage of the United States – A Short History
John Adams – A Short Biography
In the Footsteps of Columbus (Annotated) Introduction and Biography Included (with Annie J. Cannon)
Alexander Hamilton – Illustrated and Annotated (with Charles A. Conant)
Harlow Shapley – Biography of an Astronomer
Alexander Hamilton – A Short Biography
The Great Depression – A Short History
Jesse Owens, Adolf Hitler and the 1936 Summer Olympics
Thomas Jefferson– A Short Biography
Gold of My Father – A Short Tale of Adventure
Making Your Money Grow with Dividend Paying Stocks – Revised Edition

The French and Indian War – A Short History

The Mathematician John Forbes Nash Jr. – A Short Biography

The British Prime Minister Margaret Thatcher – A Short Biography

Vice President Mike Pence – A Short Biography

President Jimmy Carter – A Short Biography

President Ronald Reagan – A Short Biography

President George H. W. Bush – A Short Biography

Dr. Robert H. Goddard – A Brief Biography - Father of American Rocketry and the Space Age

Richard Nixon: A Short Biography - 37th President of the United States

Charles Lindbergh: A Short Biography - Famed Aviator and Environmentalist

Dr. Wernher von Braun: A Short Biography - Pioneer of Rocketry and Space Exploration

Bill Clinton: A Short Biography – 42nd President of the United States

Joe Biden: A Short Biography - 47th Vice President of the United States

Donald Trump: A Short Biography - 45th President of the United States

Nicolaus Copernicus: A Short Biography - The Astronomer Who Moved the Earth

America's Second War of Independence: A Short History of the War of 1812

John Quincy Adams: A Short Biography - Sixth President of the United States

Andrew Jackson: A Short Biography: Seventh President of the United States

Albert Einstein: A Short Biography Father of the Theory of Relativity

Franklin Delano Roosevelt: A Short Biography: Thirty-Second President of the United States

James Clerk Maxwell: A Short Biography: Giant of Nineteenth-Century Physics

Ernest Rutherford: A Short Biography: The Father of Nuclear Physics

Sir William Crookes: A Short Biography: Nineteenth-Century British Chemist and Spiritualist

The Journey of Apollo 11 to the Moon

William Henry Harrison: A Short Biography: Ninth President of the United States

John Tyler: A Short Biography: Tenth President of the United States

James K. Polk: A Short Biography: Eleventh President of the United States

Louisa Catherine Adams: A Short Biography: First Lady of the United States

Index

Aristarchus, 2, 19, 20

Aristarchus of Samos, 2, 19

Aristotle, 8, 19, 20, 35, 40

Averroes, 8

Bible, 28, 34

Bologna University, 9, 41

Brahe, Tycho, 38

Brudzewski, Albert, 8

Cathedral School at Włocławek, 7

Commentariolus, 24

Copernicus, Nicolaus, 1, 2, 4, 5, 6, 7, 8, 14, 19, 27, 36, 37, 40, 41, 49

Cracow, 5, 7, 8, 9, 25, 41

Dantiscus, Johannes, 18

De revolutionibus orbium coelestium, 2, 12

Disputationes adversus astrologianm divinatricenm, 11

Domenico Maria Novara da Ferrara, 10

Earth, i, ii, 2, 3, 5, 19, 20, 22, 23, 24, 27, 30, 34, 38, 39, 40, 45, 49

Epitoma in Almagestum Ptolemaei, 11

Ferber, Warmia Mauritius, 18

Ferrara, 13, 42

Frombork, 15, 16, 17, 36, 41, 42, 44

Galileo, 28, 39, 40, 45, 48

heliocentric theory, 3, 20, 22, 24, 26, 27, 28, 31, 32, 33, 34, 42, 43

Hipparchus, 19

Ibn al-Shāṭir, 21

Kepler, Johannes, 16, 32, 38, 44

Lidzbark-Warminski, 14

Locationes mansorum desertorum, 17

Monetae cudendae ratio, 18

Naṣīr al-Dīn al-Ṭūsī, 21

Newton, Isaac, 40, 48

Osiander, Andreas, 31, 44

Poland, 5, 9, 15, 37, 41

Ptolemy, 10, 11, 19, 20, 22, 25, 29, 33, 35, 40

Rheticus, 28, 29, 31, 32, 36, 43

Roman Catholic Church, 20, 34, 44

Schönberg, Nikolaus von, 26, 43

Sun, 2, 12, 16, 19, 22, 23, 24, 25, 27, 29, 30, 31, 34, 38, 39, 40

Thorn, 5, 41

University of Padua, 13, 42

Upsala University, 37

Watzenrode, Barbara, 5

Made in United States
Troutdale, OR
04/23/2024

19343691R00040